Everyone Has a
Home

Nancy Kelly Allen

Educational Media

rourkeeducationalmedia.com

Teaching Focus:

Labels and Captions- How do the labels and captions help you as you read this book?

Before Reading:

Building Academic Vocabulary and Background Knowledge

Before reading a book, it is important to set the stage for your child or student by using pre-reading strategies. This will help them develop their vocabulary, increase their reading comprehension, and make connections across the curriculum.

1. *Read the title and look at the cover. Let's make predictions about what this book will be about.*
2. *Take a picture walk by talking about the pictures/photographs in the book. Implant the vocabulary as you take the picture walk. Be sure to talk about the text features such as headings, the Table of Contents, glossary, bolded words, captions, charts/diagrams, or index.*
3. *Have students read the first page of text with you then have students read the remaining text.*
4. *Strategy Talk – use to assist students while reading.*
   - *Get your mouth ready*
   - *Look at the picture*
   - *Think…does it make sense*
   - *Think…does it look right*
   - *Think…does it sound right*
   - *Chunk it – by looking for a part you know*
5. *Read it again.*
6. *After reading the book complete the activities below.*

Content Area Vocabulary
Use glossary words in a sentence.

dome
gels
igloos
stilts
sod
tent

After Reading:

Comprehension and Extension Activity

After reading the book, work on the following questions with your child or students in order to check their level of reading comprehension and content mastery.

1. *What kinds of tools are needed to build some of the homes in the book? (Infer)*
2. *What type of home do you live in? Which home would you like to live in? (Text to self connection)*
3. *Are homes only built on land? Explain. (Asking questions)*
4. *Why do you think some homes in Norway have grass on the roof? (Infer)*

Extension Activity

Create an inspiration board, model, or plan for your future home. Using pictures from magazines, the Internet, and various art and craft supplies, create a picture or model of your future home. Share your home design with classmates, teachers, or parents.

Is your dream home a treehouse?

Around the world, many people live in homes made of brick, wood, or stone.

People also live in different types of homes.

In New Guinea, some people build homes in the tops of trees.

In Panama, some homes are built on **stilts** in the water.

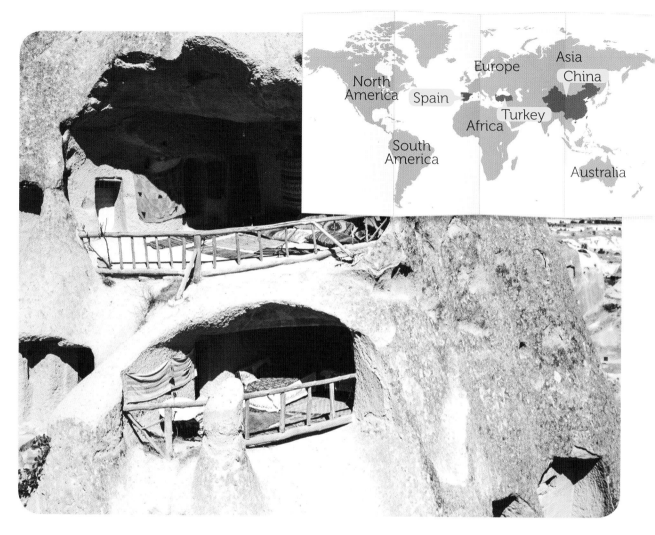

People have lived in cave homes for thousands of years. These homes are cut out of stone.

Millions of people in China live in caves.

People in Turkey and Spain live in caves, too.

Igloos are homes built with blocks of snow. Some people in Greenland, Iceland, and Alaska live in igloos.

Snow homes are in the shape of a **dome**.

A gel is a **tent**-like house in the shape of a circle.

In Mongolia, people move **gels** from one place to another by using camels.

Africa

In Africa, China, and other parts of the world, mud is used to build houses.

Clay mud is mixed with straw to make strong walls.

In Vietnam, some homes float on the water.

The Netherlands also has a community of floating homes.

In Bolivia, some houses are shaped like acorns. The walls are made of clumps of roots and dirt.

Roofs made of grass, called **sod**, cover some homes in Norway.

All around the world, homes are built in different shapes and sizes. Many homes stay in one place. Others move from place to place.

The homes look different, but in some ways they are alike. All are places for families to eat, sleep, and live.

Photo Glossary

 **dome** (dohm): Shaped like half of a ball.

 **gels** (jelz): Houses that are covered with felt cloth.

 **igloos** (IG-looz): Houses built with blocks of snow.

stilts (stiltz): Poles or posts.

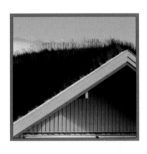

sod (sahd): Grass and dirt.

tent (tehnt): A portable house that can be disassembled and moved.

Index

Show What You Know

1. Why do people build different types of homes?
2. How are homes alike?
3. What are some different types of homes?

Websites to Visit

www.kids.usa.gov/social-studies

www.discoverykids.com/games/room-maker

www.abcya.com/build_a_house.htm

About the Author

Nancy Kelly Allen lives in Kentucky. Her house is among the trees, but it's not a treehouse. Part of it is underground, but it's not a cave. It is surrounded by sod but none is on the roof. She lives in a log cabin with her husband, Larry, and two little dogs, Jazi and Roxi.

Meet The Author!
www.meetREMauthors.com

© 2016 Rourke Educational Media

www.rourkeeducationalmedia.com

PHOTO CREDITS: Cover: © Nejron Photo, Rajesh Patabiraman; Title Page: © Joel Carillet; Page 3: © designpics; Page 4: © majana; Page 5: © Lee Rogers; Page 6: © Sergey Vryadnikov; Page 7: © ildogesto, Vilainecrevette; Page 8: © irinabogomolova; Page 9: © Corbis - How Hwee Young; Page 10: © Ivan Kmit; Page 11: © Marteric; Page 12: © Bartosz Hadyniak; Page 13: © Davor Lovincic; Page 14: © appletreegirl; Page 15 © Jakrit Jiraratwao; Page 16 © 12ee12; Page 17: © Dutch Scenery; Page 18 © Viaje al corazón - Wikipedia; Page 19: © mirisek; Page 20: © Peeter Vilsimaa; Page 21: © Christopher Futcher

Edited by: Keli Sipperley

Cover and Interior design by: Tara Raymo

Library of Congress PCN Data

Everyone Has a Home / Nancy Kelly Allen
(Little World Everyone Everywhere)
ISBN (hard cover)(alk. paper) 978-1-63430-365-1
ISBN (soft cover) 978-1-63430-465-8
ISBN (e-Book) 978-1-63430-562-4
Library of Congress Control Number: 2015931702

Printed in the United States of America, North Mankato, Minnesota

Also Available as:

ROURKE'S
e-Books